THE SICILIAN LIGHTHOUSE

OTHER WORKS BY CAROLE DI TOSTI

NOVEL
Peregrine: The Ceremony of Powers

POETRY BOOK
Light Shifts

PLAY
The Berglarian

THEATER AND FILM REVIEWS
(On the following sites)
Sandi Durell's Theater Pizzazz.com
Blogcritics.org
Carole Di Tosti's NYC Skyline

ESSAYS/OPINION PIECES
The Fat and the Skinny on Wellness.com

WEBSITE
www.caroleditostibooks.com

For William

Acknowledgements

The Sicilian Lighthouse has not yet been produced. It was directed in Zoom readings during the COVID-19 pandemic by Kae Fujisawa, whose guidance has proven invaluable. I would like to thank the following actors for their time and effort at rehearsals and presentations of scenes of *The Sicilian Lighthouse*. These especially helped in the play's development process: Jody Moore, Byron O'Hanlon, Leyla Hadi, Drew Stone, Emmett O'Connell, Tony Macy-Perez, Virginia Gregory, Kolbe Handal, Wendy Kornreich and Dylan T. Jackson. Thanks go to the following individuals for their feedback at workshops and private readings of *The Sicilian Lighthouse*: Gail Botta, Camille Block, Rosary O'Neill, Suzanne Bradbeer, Billie Roe, Gayle Greene, Mary Fassino, Nicholas Priore, Nan Ewing, Andrea Harris, Emily Suzuki. A special thanks goes to renowned playwright and playwriting teacher and friend Eduardo Machado, for his wisdom, humor and great good will toward writers and the creative process. *The Sicilian Lighthouse* was conceived in his class.

THE SICILIAN LIGHTHOUSE

A COMEDY

CAROLE DI TOSTI

The Sicilian Lighthouse: A Comedy
Published: December 2023
Printed in the United States of America
ISBN: 978-1-7359752-9-0

ALL RIGHTS RESERVED. Except for brief passages quoted in newspaper, magazine, radio or television reviews, no part of this book may be reproduced in any form or by any means, electronic or mechanical, including photocopying or recording, or by an information storage and retrieval system, without permission in writing from the publisher.

Professionals and amateurs are hereby warned that this material, being fully protected under the Copyright Laws of the United States of America and all other countries of the Berne and Universal Copyright Conventions, is subject to a royalty. All rights, including by not limited to, professional, amateur, recording, motion picture, recitation, lecturing, public reading, radio and television broadcasting, and the rights of translation into foreign languages are expressly reserved. Particular emphasis is placed on the question of readings and all uses of this book by educational institutions, permission for which must be secured from Carole Di Tosti, A Priori Publishing, 8333 118th St. Kew Gardens, NY 11415.

DISCLAIMER: This is a work of fiction. Names, characters, businesses, places, events and incidents are either the products of the author's imagination or used in a fictitious manner. Any resemblance to actual persons, living or dead, or actual events is purely coincidental.

The Sicilian Lighthouse is published by A Priori Publishing, 8333 118th St. Kew Gardens, NY 11415

Copyright ©2023 by Carole Di Tosti
Image on next page by Rochak Shukla on Freepik

CHARACTERS

CARL FILIPPO, filmmaker, son of Maria and Tony (20s)
MARIA FILIPPO, second wife of Tony, mother of Carl (50s)
TONY FILIPPO, father of Pedro and Carl (60s)
PEDRO FILIPPO, half-brother of Carl (30s)
MILA HANSON, Carl's girlfriend (30s)
LAWYER PAUL TROTTO, Tony's lawyer for the restaurant (60s)
NURSE, a nurse working the night shift in the Emergency Room
ALONZO, Trotto's operative
POLICE OFFICERS (2 friends of Pedro's, impersonating cops)
EMT, FIREMEN, ASSORTED

SPIRITS

ERMINIA FILIPPO, Tony's deceased first wife, Pedro's mother
NONNO CARLO, Tony's father, Carl's grandfather
TONY'S GHOST, a younger, refreshed Tony

SETTING

TIME: Present
PLACE: In and around Jersey City, NJ and Manhattan, NY

Act One

Scene 1 The Filippo's Jersey City, NJ townhouse and The Sicilian Lighthouse, Manhattan, NY.
Scene 2 Manhattan hospital ER and hospital parking lot.
Scene 3 The Filippo's Jersey City townhouse.
Scene 4 Vecchio Funeral Home in Jersey City.
Scene 5 Lawyer Trotto's office in Queens, NY.
Scene 6 Mila's Manhattan loft.
Scene 7 Lawyer Trotto's office in Queens.
Scene 8 Maria's Jersey City townhouse and Flashback to the Argentine Club, Manhattan.
Scene 9 Maria's Jersey City townhouse living room and the upstairs apartment.
Scene 10 Maria's Jersey City townhouse

Act Two

Scene 1 Mila's Manhattan loft
Scene 2 Maria's Jersey City townhouse
Scene 3 The Sicilian Lighthouse
Scene 4 The Sicilian Lighthouse Ristorante

ACT ONE

Scene 1

Present day in a townhouse apartment in Jersey City. In his bedroom Carl gets dressed. His father Tony walks in on him.

TONY You have to open up.

CARL I can't.

TONY Why?

CARL I have a film shoot.

TONY Postpone it until tomorrow when Patrick can cover.

CARL Everyone's lined up. Can't reschedule.

TONY Don't do this to me.

CARL I marked it here on the calendar. Did you look at it?

TONY I never look at that thing.

CARL Easier for you to abuse my time.

TONY Calendars make no sense.

CARL You intentionally forgot. And refuse to be reminded.

TONY I didn't forget. No one can cover.

CARL Not my problem.

MARIA What's going on?

TONY   He's not opening.

MARIA   This is our bread and butter.

CARL   So, hire a barman. I told him a hundred times. I have a shoot.

TONY   Do both. Open, then shoot.

CARL   No time. I'm picking up some actors.

MARIA   In the city? I bet she'll be there.

CARL   "She" has a name.

MARIA (*mutters*)   Vieja.

CARL   Don't insult her.

TONY   What does she have to do with it?

MARIA   An excuse to see her and have sex.

CARL   You refuse to believe I'm a filmmaker. I've stopped caring.

TONY   The chances of you becoming a filmmaker are 5% yes, 105% never.

CARL   Your math stinks. All sense knocked out of you when Max convinced you that taking over a full-on restaurant was the same as running a pizza joint.

TONY   You're the dreamer.

CARL   I know the difference between what I can do and what I can't. You don't.

MARIA   Get Pedro to cover.

The Sicilian Lighthouse

TONY He's painting. At least he's making a living while this bum lives off us.

CARL You call living off your wife's nursing salary making a living?

MARIA Suggesting he cover is a big step for me.

CARL His mother must be turning over in her sainted grave.

MARIA If you commit suicide, you don't get to be buried in sanctified church ground. Not a sainted grave.

CARL All the more reason she's churning up golf turf. That's where she's buried, isn't she, near Ivana Trump on the golf course? She's ten feet away from *Trump Links* in that quasi pet cemetery where people are buried with their pets isn't she? Ha, ha, ha.

TONY She's overlooking the water like she wanted. YOU open up. It's not Pedro's job.

CARL You support his painting but not my films. He paints cats and dogs.

TONY People pay good money for portraits of their pets.

CARL They don't even look like anything. Whoever heard of abstract animals? Two squares and 5 black lines represent Timmy the terrier. Oh, here's an improvement. A black square and two yellow lines for Marilyn the Maltese. I'd buy a fake Rothko over those pieces of shit any day.

TONY You can't afford a fake Rothko.

CARL My short about COVID was accepted in 5 film festivals. It's real art.

TONY Whoever heard of Lakewood Film Festival in Iowa?

CARL Accepted at Sarasota Film Festival.

TONY Did it win?

CARL Acceptances are looked at as wins.

TONY If you don't win, nobody cares.

CARL I said an acceptance is a win.

MARIA No one wants to see a film about what we suffered through that nearly ended the business. Uh! See my documentary about dying of COVID.

CARL Why can't you support me?

MARIA We support your film addiction every day you stay here. You have to give us something back or marry your M.I.L.F.

CARL Since when did you get crude?

MARIA Since the $100,000 hasn't been paid on this month's lease and fines for The Sicilian Lighthouse.

CARL Running late. Mom, you do the drinks.

TONY No way. She put Jamison instead of Bacardi in the Long Island Iced Tea. That hedge fund guy nearly choked to death.

CARL You mean the quant from Buenos Aires who likes our morcillas? A Long Island Iced Tea is a loser drink to impress a date. (*laughs*) Serves him right, the "big man." (*mutters*) Asshole.

TONY A faithful customer your mother nearly blew out the door. I had to comp his dinners.

CARL This film will be even bigger than my winning short at Sarasota.

MARIA It didn't win and you're going backward.

CARL Don't you understand what indie filmmakers go through without a film school backing them?

TONY I don't want to hear about how we didn't pay for your film school, and you went into debt and dropped out. Lennie the Lux gives better returns on his loans than the bank loans you're paying high interest on for your losing college proposition. So now you're here and not in Los Angeles. Deal with it.

CARL Cut me some slack.

TONY You owe me a month. No days off.

CARL That's twenty-five days.

TONY Monday and Tuesday's off. Added to what you already owe us for your film fantasy.

CARL Aren't parents supposed to support their kids, give them a leg up?

MARIA We gave you a leg, then the other leg, then an arm. You cut us some slack. Your answer is the M.I.L.F.

CARL She's not a mother.

TONY (*laughs*) A Jaguar motherfucker.

CARL You can't even get the feline right! If you want to insult her, insult her with the right meme. Cougar. Cougar!

TONY What's the difference? All pussies are the same.

CARL I hope you drop dead!

MARIA He can't! (*laughs*) Without him we'd go bankrupt. I don't know how to run a restaurant!

Lights dim. Seamless segue to lights up later that evening, closing time same day in the Sicilian Lighthouse restaurant in Manhattan, N.Y. Tony is cleaning up. Carl enters.

TONY You're useless! We closed.

CARL I stopped the shoot early to be here to help you.

TONY Your mother made a mess of things. I have to straighten it out. You'll make it worse!

CARL You look exhausted doing double duty. I've closed before. I'm here to help.

TONY I have to do it. Go to your puttana.

CARL Mom! Take him home. I'm closing.

TONY Get out! Get out! Useless. You're not getting near the money drawer. ARGH! ARGH! AWK, AWK, AWK!

Tony collapses. Carl kneels next to him.

CARL Dad, Dad. (*pause*) Mom! Anyone. Call 911! Sammy, call 911. I think it's a heart attack!

Spotlight dims and scene shifts.

Scene 2

Lights rise on the ER at 1:30 AM. The curtained off area. Under a sheet is a body. Carl paces, tries to relax stretching his arms, neck. Mila rushes in.

CARL   Thanks for coming. You're saving my life.

MILA   How is he?

CARL   He's, he's... Mom left in tears and went home to smoke some pot. They refused to give her a sedative.

MILA   Can I see him? I want to pray.

CARL   I don't know.

MILA   I'll pray and lay hands. They can come back, you know.

CARL   I don't want him to come back if he's brain dead.

MILA   Don't say that. Sometimes they can rise. If they're not ready to leave this plane of existence. You don't know unless you let me try.

The nurse comes in. She looks at Carl.

NURSE   What's going on here?

CARL   It's OK. She wants to pray.

MILA *(as if in a trance, swaying)*   I feel, I feel him hovering. He's watching us. His presence is heavy with life, even yet.

NURSE   Are you family?

CARL   She's with me. Yes. I called her to help.

NURSE He's gone. She can't help. We did all we could.

MILA You don't know. There are moments of hovering between...life and death. (*pause*) Humpf! You look too dull to know the difference between real spirit life and dead as a doornail death.

NURSE (*angry*) Only immediate family are allowed with the body.

CARL It's OK. I authorize her to be here.

NURSE Why wasn't she here with the others?

CARL She hit traffic. She couldn't help it.

NURSE It's not protocol. You have no power to authorize anything.

MILA I'm praying over him.

NURSE Are you one of those resurrection people who hang around hospitals? No. No, No. You have to leave!

CARL Please! One last goodbye. Please...

NURSE Just for a minute. Then you go.

Nurse exists.

MILA Come, over to the bed.

CARL I can't look at him.

Mila throws herself on top of the body.

MILA (*dramatically*) You don't have to leave, Mr. Filippo. If you want to rise up, you can. The Lord lets you decide. He always gives you a second chance. In the Name of Jesus Christ of Nazareth. Rise!

Nurse enters.

NURSE (*angry*)   That's enough.

CARL   Mila. Let's go.

MILA   If I pray in tongues, deeply. He'll respond!

NURSE   I can't have this. Others need the bed. He's going to the morgue.

MILA (*angry*)   You're so nasty! We're grieving here! Grieving! You know the word grieving? Don't interfere with God!

CARL (*takes her by the arm*)   Mila, come on. Let's not make a scene. There's nothing more to be done.

MILA (*forcefully to the Nurse*)   This is on you!

NURSE (*sarcastic*)   It is. He must be autopsied. Now!

Carl and Mila leave. Outside the hospital.

CARL   Stay the night.

MILA   Not with your mother. She despises me.

CARL   I can't be alone in the house with her. And…I'm afraid of him.

MILA   What do you mean?

CARL   He'll come for me. We had a horrible fight. I caused this. I told him to drop dead.

MILA I touched his spirit. You said you didn't want him to come back. So, he couldn't.

CARL I'm glad. And I'm not glad.

MILA I opened the door for him. The nurse slammed it shut. She's the devil or it's not God's will.

CARL Both.

MILA Let's go to my place.

CARL What do I tell my mother?

MILA It's your life. You choose, not her.

CARL She needs me. Why don't you sleep in the apartment upstairs? I'll sneak up.

MILA She knows we're together. Expects us to sleep together. Just come up.

CARL Why did he have to drop dead now? In the middle of my film shoot.

MILA You told him to drop dead. For once he accommodated you.

CARL You have to stay with me. Please. I love you.

MILA I'll have to get my things. Drive back from Manhattan. Cancel my plans.

CARL I'm afraid for what lies ahead. The wake, the funeral, the cemetery, his ghost...

MILA Call the pastor at the church we went to that time. He has a peaceful manner and he's so understanding and sweet.

CARL His last words to me. "You're useless. Get out!"

MILA You're not useless, never useless to me.

Mila kisses him. He hugs her as the lights dim.

Scene 3

It is 8 AM next day in the kitchen of the family's Jersey apartment. Pedro, Carl's half-brother, who is 10 years older, confronts Carl.

PEDRO He collapsed during an argument? You and her always stressed him. You are ungrateful and selfish!

CARL Oh, the golden boy. You wouldn't let him forget that your mom chose death over him. You tortured him about her suicide.

PEDRO You squeezed his heart. He couldn't breathe.

Mila enters. She sees them and tries to distract them.

MILA Shall I make coffee?

CARL You fuck. Don't dump this on mom and me.

MARIA No fighting until we get through these next days. Then you can tear each other to bits. No Tony to get between you anymore. Kill each other for all I care. Tony's laughing in heaven.

PEDRO Pop faked believing in God to please you. He's not laughing. He's in oblivion.

MILA Thank you for letting me use the upstairs apartment, Mrs. Filippo.

MARIA No problem. Happy you are here to comfort Carl after what he did.

CARL Mom...

PEDRO You pulled the trigger.

CARL Don't confuse me with you.

MARIA "I hope you drop dead." I heard you say it.

CARL He didn't drop dead right away. He waited until I came back to help. Then he dropped dead in front of me to make me feel guilty.

MARIA It happened. You didn't cause it...

CARL He had a choice. He never went to the doctor for check-ups. He was exhausted. He had a bad night, couldn't sleep. The restaurant was messed up.

MARIA It was a stroke.

PEDRO Whatever. You asked for an autopsy. You'll see he had Alzheimer's like my wife says.

MARIA It doesn't matter. Bills to pay. The restaurant can't open for a few days. There's no one to take over.

CARL I can.

MARIA Maybe you, Pedro?

PEDRO Maybe.

MARIA Anyway, I'm going back to Argentina.

CARL What?

MILA This is family business. I'll go home.

MARIA No. Stay. Hear what this family is like when they face tragedy. Decide if you want to be with Carl, the lost child. When a beloved dies, the storm comes. Confusion, darkness. The vultures pick the dead man's bones.

CARL No one's a vulture here.

MARIA But there IS something to pick over.

MILA I lost my Dad unexpectedly like your husband, your father. No words describe it. Even if they're sick for a long time like my father. You think you're prepared. You're never prepared.

CARL I told him. But he wouldn't go to the doctor.

PEDRO You let him take over the loser restaurant, despite me telling him not to. Then, you all fucked it up. I wash my hands of this.

CARL And when he needed you to cover yesterday, you painted your stray cats. It's on YOUR head!

PEDRO It was a Doberman, a rich client.

CARL You always refused to help him with The Lighthouse, or anything connected with it.

PEDRO Anything that's ours in the restaurant goes to pay off the lease. If you hadn't come back to upset him, he'd be alive. We'd have the money.

MARIA Your mother hated me. I'm sorry she let you down. You were 17 when you ran away to Taos with that puta. Then you met your wife. And you moved here because she could get a higher salary working in a private hospital to support you. No words about how you live your life. No words about how Carl can't live off his depressing films no one likes. You lost a father. I lost a husband. Your daughter lost her grandfather. It's time to think about what he meant to us. Time to look through pictures and see the days of happiness. (*pause*) Mila, be a good girl and go to the bakery around the corner. Get some sweet rolls for breakfast.

Mila leaves as lights dim.

Scene 4

It is one day later in the Vecchio Funeral Home vestibule. Dressed in black, Pedro sits scowling on the back of a sofa, shoes in the seating area. Carl and Mila, also in black, stand waiting.

CARL I'm glad Pastor Amate is here to calm things.

MILA His prayers help me.

CARL Mom will be happy to hear him talk about Jesus. He will ward off Pedro's evil eye (*laughs near hysteria*).

MILA Pedro looks like he's ready to pounce.

CARL It's a constant battle between us. Maria can't stop it. Her words slide off him like grease.

PASTOR AMATE Are we ready? I met your mom, very sweet. And your sister-in-law. We prayed for Tony like your mom wanted. Your brother won't talk to me. Black clouds fly over his head.

CARL He IS the black cloud (*laughs maniacally*).

MILA Are you OK, Babe?

PASTOR AMATE God showed me. The spirit of darkness is trying to take over. Our prayers lift it. For a time.

CARL I can't say anything but insults. Pedro made Dad feel guilty about his mom's suicide. I bet Dad tried to make it up to Pedro in the will. I dread going to the lawyer next week. I dread today, and the church service and the cemetery. Dread is the right word. But I never understood what it meant until now.

Mila kisses him on the cheek. Comforts him.

PASTOR AMATE   Let's go in. Pedro, come and join us. Pay respects to your father.

PEDRO   He's dead and gone. And he never believed in God. You people can't even honor or respect him for his beliefs. Or his wishes. He never wanted a wake. He never wanted a big funeral. Never! On this day you dishonor him. (*angry*) Outrageous!

The others exit, leaving Pedro on the couch scowling as lights dim.

Scene 5

It is the following week. Pedro, Maria, Carl sit in front of Trotto's desk. Pedro sits away from Carl.

MARIA Are you sure there's no other will?

PAUL TROTTO Yes.

MARIA He left out Carl.

TROTTO As long as he didn't leave you out.

CARL I expected it.

MARIA That's because he wanted us to be together. When we discussed retiring in Buenos Aires, all of us would go.

CARL That was when I was younger, and he was in better shape.

PEDRO Mi padre. He never forgot I loved him. I am the first. He would never cut me out of his will.

MARIA He felt guilty. This was your payoff. To get you off his back.

CARL He gave you and mom percentages of The Lighthouse because I never wanted to be there.

TROTTO In the last part of the will, the house goes to you, Mrs. Filippo.

MARIA The contents?

TROTTO You have to decide amongst yourselves. Maybe Pedro wants to take a few things of his father's.

CARL My father meant nothing to Pedro apart from his assets. His mother committed suicide to punish Tony. Pedro was a casualty of that disastrous marriage.

PEDRO You don't speak for me. You don't define my life.

MARIA He wanted a divorce. She had a better plan. Haunt him forever by killing herself.

CARL Italy vs. Argentina with your mom, not mine. He and mom got along and had a great marriage.

PEDRO If you hadn't weaseled your way into his arms, they would have worked it out. But he couldn't resist putas.

Carl stands up.

CARL Take that back! Take that back!

PEDRO The truth? I never lie for others!

TROTTO I'm a black belt. I'll deck you both with roundhouse kicks. We're almost done. Sit.

PEDRO He honored me and mom by giving me 80% of The Lighthouse. Remember that. (*disgust*) He made Maria an irrelevance.

CARL You can come up with the $100,000 you'll need to pay off the lease and fines and keep it solvent? Ah, ha, ha! NOPE!

MARIA So when does this happen?

TROTTO If you and Pedro agree, he can take over, run the restaurant now. Or you take it over.

Carl sits back in the chair.

CARL Don't expect me to be barman. Either of you!

MARIA I can show you the books. Where he kept the merchant lists for orders, maintenance, staff. I can help you until you get on your feet. Or we sell the contents that belong to the LLC and pay off the lease.

PEDRO I want to run it. This is the purpose I've been looking for. I know the staff. I'll make a great restaurateur. I have some ideas.

CARL Ideas? Set up your easel and do your clients' pet portraits as they dine? Ah, ha, ha, ha.

PEDRO Not a bad idea.

CARL Change the name and call it The Pet House!

MARIA Stop it!

CARL Where were you the night he died? The night he needed you most?

PEDRO I never felt comfortable when you all were there. Now, it's different. I'm free to make decisions without you people screaming.

MARIA So, about the house...

TROTTO You have sole ownership. Pay the bills, rent the apartment, pay the taxes and upkeep, stay or sell. Carl gets nothing unless he's with you.

PEDRO Can she cede her 20% of the restaurant to me?

TROTTO You need a separate contract between you two to buy her out.

CARL What if I don't agree?

PEDRO Didn't you hear the man? Pop cut you out.

TROTTO If you keep it as is, she gets 20% of the profits the restaurant makes monthly.

PEDRO So, I'm working and slaving and sweating and have to give her the 20%?

CARL Run the restaurant. Paint abstracts of that rich quant's Borzoi to stay liquid. Ha, ha, Ha.

PEDRO Maria, we have to talk. When do you need to know about the restaurant?

TROTTO After probate. It's a separate contract. Now, the life insurance policy.

MARIA	**PEDRO**
Well?	Glad to hear it!

TROTTO The money is released immediately.

MARIA It's to me, right?

PEDRO Vulture's picking the dead man's bones…

CARL You're one to talk. You want 100% of the PET HOUSE. You sit there, a sniveling rat complaining about my mother! Her pedigree is known. Who was YOUR grandfather? Another suicide?

MARIA You want a deal, Pedro? Be civil or I'll take the 20% while you run it into the ground.

PEDRO She's liable for the debts, too, right?

TROTTO No. If you want to run it, it's on your head. She's a passive partner. Uninvolved. She only gets 20% of the profits, not the liabilities.

PEDRO Outrageous.

MARIA The life insurance?

TROTTO All of it goes to Carl.

CARL (*to Pedro*) Fuck you. Pop didn't forget me.

TROTTO It's with a stipulation, or you get nothing.

CARL Christ.

TROTTO You have to use it for the University of Buenos Aires while you live with your mom in the house she buys there.

CARL	**PEDRO**
INSANE!	HA, HA, HA, HA.

CARL He's reaching from beyond the grave to choke me!

MARIA All of us. Stipulations and conditions.

PEDRO Except for the house.

MARIA Which is mine and Carl's

PEDRO He cut out Carl.

MARIA It's my choice to cut him in. He's my son. Maybe I'll give him half of the house money to spite you. But I don't have your mother's evil spirit. I'm kinder.

TROTTO You do that, and the will can be contested by Pedro. If the conditions are not followed in one element, it's a trigger to void the will. Then the fight really begins.

CARL He knew what he was doing. The hell he caused in his life continues, and he gets to watch.

PEDRO He was an atheist. He's in the great vacuum. He did this to force us to get along.

MARIA Ha, ha, ha, ha	**CARL** Ha, ha, ha, ha

PEDRO You're supposed to be Christians, aren't you? Act like it, or you're a fucking bunch of hypocrites.

MARIA May I use your restroom?

TROTTO Through there.

Maria leaves momentarily to take something to soothe her nerves.

PEDRO Mama's boy. He knew you'd never leave her. He just made it a fact.

CARL I'm Italian. The Argentinians stay with mama, except when mama kills herself.

Maria returns. There's a skunk smell following her. Pedro sniffs her, he rolls his eyes.

PEDRO *(disdainful)* Aren't you a little old for weed?

MARIA *(to Pedro)* Humpff! I've been thinking. Can Carl cede the life insurance money to me since it's ready cash?

TROTTO Maybe, but it'll cost you to set up a contract.

CARL It isn't much, right?

PEDRO It's enough. Zopilote!

CARL How much?

TROTTO What's a zopilote?

CARL No fucking idea.	**PEDRO** A greedy buzzard.

CARL I don't want what goes with the insurance money. I visited Argentina a few times. Except for Lucy, hated it. It's no place for me.

TROTTO It's $300,000. You have a lot of decisions.

MARIA I feel safer making the decisions here, right now.

CARL I have to think.

PEDRO I have to tell Patty that I won't be babysitting at home. I'll be at The Lighthouse.

TROTTO I trust you'll come to an agreement.

CARL Don't. This is war. We're fighting ourselves and each other. Dad fired the first shot when he collapsed.

MARIA Is there a place where we might discuss this?

TROTTO No one is in the conference room now.

MARIA I'm the executrix of the estate, am I not?

TROTTO No. I'm the executor. Tony left me in charge as an old friend. If you can't agree to the terms, then it can go to mediation. Then you would each have to get your own lawyer.

CARL How bully of you.

TROTTO It's not like we're talking millions. It's chump change.

PEDRO To you. But it's our lives.

TROTTO He wanted you to agree.

MARIA Obviously.

CARL Control freak.

PEDRO (*screams*) He's dead! You'll never see him again! Can't you be happy for that?

TROTTO The grieving process is different for everyone. Families explode when the will is read.

MARIA Let's discuss the conditions privately.

PEDRO We stay here. In there, I'll give Mama's boy a black eye. You're too weak to stop me.

CARL Your mama's Patty, 'cause she wears the money pants.

TROTTO Another option is that Maria takes out a mortgage on your house for $150,000 and pays off the lease and invests what's left in restaurant upgrades.

CARL Mom. Give me half the $300,000 so I can just get out of your hair. You take the house. I'll use the money for my film.

TROTTO Pedro can contest it.

CARL What the fuck?

TROTTO You change any of the conditions, then the other parties that have been excluded can contest it and throw the will into the vacuum. Contested, the best lawyer wins.

MARIA You mean we agree, or the lawyers get it all in fees?

TROTTO That's the way things work.

CARL He knew we would never agree. You helped him.

TROTTO When we drew up the will, we went over every stipulation. I made condition upon condition.

MARIA Then we have to compromise. We must try to get along.

PEDRO (*manic laughter*) Ha, ha, ha, ah. Ha, ha.

CARL Can it, you fuck.

PEDRO Brilliant. He's dead. But he lives on in our hatred for each other and in our fights whether we agree or not. There will always be disagreements.

MARIA I'm ready to give it all to the lawyers. What's money in exchange for the misery of fighting?

PEDRO My new life.

CARL My films getting made.

MARIA Going home. Seeing my sister and nieces and nephews.

CARL You see them every year.

MARIA It's different being around family. Here it was just you and Tony.

PEDRO Maria, you don't want to hassle with me. I'll be nasty if you look over my shoulder with the restaurant.

CARL Mama Patty will be happy you run The Lighthouse and finally be a man.

PEDRO There may never be a profit. I'll be slaving 14 hours like Dad did to be in debt with nothing to show for it.

CARL How will Mom know you're not lying and embezzling money, unless she sees the books?

MARIA I can't take the stress. Do I have to look at the books and be involved?

TROTTO Technically no. You could appoint me to work with the accountant as the overseer.

PEDRO I can make it without you.

CARL You can't make a likeness of a chihuahua.

PEDRO Difficult to draw. Nasty yappers.

MARIA The place is in arrears. You have to borrow money to pay off the lease and the fines or sell the contents. And at auction the contents won't pay it off.

PEDRO So?

CARL You have credit? Your house is in Patty's name, right? She'll let you borrow against it?

PEDRO Of course. Everything we have, we own together.

CARL Ha, ha, ha ha. Bullshit.

TROTTO Another option is that Maria takes out a mortgage on your house for $100,000 and pays off the lease and invests what's left in restaurant upgrades. In exchange for another 15%. So it would be 65% Pedro and 35% profits for Maria.

CARL She has to pay off that mortgage? With what? If I split the life insurance with her, Pedro will sue.

TROTTO Do you have any savings, Maria? Any cash stashed away anywhere?

MARIA So now I'm an entrepreneur, borrowing, selling, buying, leasing? I just want to go to Buenos Aires.

TROTTO I can manage it for you.

CARL How much?

PEDRO You get a percentage of filing court papers. A percentage of the contracts we have to make, if we go outside

◊ } The Sicilian Lighthouse ɝ ◊

Dad's conditions. A percentage of mediation fees if we contest each other. Our money shrinks. You end up getting the money Dad left us? No fucking way.

TROTTO It's a good thing he didn't make his OWN will and botch it. Equivalent to dying intestate. Probate court could appoint another lawyer who would take it all.

CARL Mom. You hold all the cards.

PEDRO Not really. We contest what anyone does that we don't like. And I'm his son. He disinherited me from his life insurance. I want one third.

MARIA Don't go there.

CARL See what he's doing? He'll be like this if you get the mortgage and pay off the lease, and then it will be something else he'll demand. Or behind your back he decides to let The Lighthouse go down, sell all the contents and just paint his grand masterpieces and fuck your 20% or 35%.

MARIA I don't agree to any of this. I don't have to.

PEDRO Su puta madre!

CARL (*calmly*) Ok, Ok. Now. You went over the line.

Carl gets up and neatly decks Pedro who tips the chair over and falls on the floor.

PEDRO I meant la puta madre...mistake, la puta...

CARL No you didn't...RATO!

Carl is all over him punching and kicking him as Trotto puts on his kung fu motions and throws Carl off Pedro kung fu style as all grapple on the floor.

27

MARIA Dios mio. Que hace, Tony? Que hace?

Maria puts her head in her hands, then lifts it in thought. She takes out a joint and smokes it. The men are too busy fighting to notice the visitation. Tony steps out from the shadows into the spotlight. Maria's too involved with taking deep breaths of perfumed smoke to see him.

TONY (*to audience*) Never underestimate the influence of an atheist when the chips are down.

Maria turns around, misses Tony who disappears. She continues smoking the joint.

Lights dim.

Scene 6

The evening of the same day, after the fight between Pedro, Maria and Carl in Trotto's office. Mila's apartment.

MILA That was the BEST!

CARL I fuck great when I'm angry.

MILA Sorry about your brawl. Happy I'm the beneficiary.

CARL Sex is what you get. I don't have money.

MILA I don't care. I'm not into men for money.

CARL (*kisses her*) Sweet exception.

MILA My first husband taught me well.

CARL Rich?

MILA In money! A pobrecito in everything else. Our life together was a hall of mirrors.

CARL You loved him.

MILA Sometimes. Then he solved the problem.

CARL By dying. (*pause*) Tony's death is my problem.

MILA It's your solution.

CARL You're my solution.

MILA A distraction before the real bullfight begins.

CARL I'll never compromise with my half-brother.

MILA Let it go for now. Anger gives birth to bad decisions.

CARL Not going with mom to Buenos Aires, unless…

MILA No.

CARL Yes.

MILA I can't imagine myself there.

CARL Why not?

MILA I don't speak Spanish good, and with a "Jo."

CARL Learn.

MILA Rosetta Stone is too slow.

CARL Live with us and pick up the language on site. Dive into the pampas.

MILA Can't swim.

CARL The best beef in the world.

MILA I prefer fish. Intend to go vegan.

CARL Don't put me off with lame jokes.

MILA If I don't joke, I'll weep. I have a career.

CARL That you hate. But the American Embassy will get you a professorship.

MILA I can't live with you.

CARL Why?

MILA With your mom? Under her roof? With her rules? Only room for one feline.

CARL It will be different if we're married.

MILA Interesting way to ask me.

CARL You don't accept it when I'm romantic.

MILA Might have been nice this time.

CARL When you have nothing of your own but debts, what can you offer but sex, youth and romance?

MILA Bullseye! OUCH!

CARL I don't care that you're older.

MILA You believe that rot about sexual peaks.

CARL Yes

MILA I'm not peaking yet. And I can't have children.

CARL Can't or won't?

MILA I won't be responsible for child abuse.

CARL Way harsh.

MILA A realist. I can't be a good mother. And if I can't, I won't be a motherfucker.

CARL Acid.

MILA I know where I can get some.

CARL I mean you're pouring acid on you and me.

MILA I won't fuck up our kids and fuck us up.

CARL I trust your parenting skills.

MILA You're being unreasonable and desperate. It's unattractive.

CARL What are you saying?

MILA Take me out of your perfect picture. Decide what you want. I'll arrange my colors after.

CARL (*pause*) I'm starving. I'll make us huevos rancheros.

MILA Don't have the ingredients. A smoothie, instead.

CARL Cooking relaxes me. It's either eggs or sex.

MILA Can't we talk about this?

CARL You just said I should decide first, then you arrange your paints.

MILA Yes, unless you want my opinion.

Silence

MILA We should pray about it. God gave me a sign about your film and your career, but I want God to confirm it.

CARL What sign?

MILA A dream.

CARL About me?

MILA You and I were in a tropical paradise, lush, verdant, exotic birds calling to each other.

The Sicilian Lighthouse

CARL My relative's garden in Buenos Aires.

MILA The birds were squawking in English.

CARL (*wry*) Ha, Ha!

MILA Your father was there. He gave me a drink.

CARL Arsenic laced marguerita?

MILA Water.

CARL Don't get it.

MILA He said, "Savor it slowly." Then he disappeared under a sailor palm tree.

CARL I don't get it.

MILA I interpret dreams. The water was cool, refreshing, like from a mountain spring.

CARL So?

MILA You.

CARL Pray some more.

MILA You are my cool, refreshing drink.

CARL You dreamed this after you went down on me? Ha, ha.

MILA You quench my thirst. After sex with other guys, I was still thirsty, hungry.

CARL You're flattering me.

MILA What if I am? It's true.

CARL   So! Dad arises from hell to show us he supports us? OK. Marry me.

MILA   He wasn't in hell. A garden.

CARL   You don't know where he is. I'll stay here.

MILA   Disinherit yourself?

CARL   I can't live with mom, obeying my father's prison conditions. Maybe your dream means he'll influence mom to sneak money to me.

MILA   Pedro will be a snake if you don't go with your mom. He'll contest the will. The lawyers will get it all.

CARL   I can fly down to Buenos Aires, stay a week and help my mother get set up. Then, fly back and live with you in secret.

MILA   What if your dad is tempting me to the abyss like Hamlet's father's ghost? I have to pray.

CARL   Whatever. Fuck breakfast. I'm hungry. You are delicious.

He kisses her passionately. Tony's ghost appears. He watches them, looks out into the audience, smiles then leaves.

Lights dim.

Scene 7

Trotto's office, two days later.

TROTTO I'm glad you decided to meet separately.

MARIA How will we know what really happens between you and Pedro?

CARL You could double cross him and us.

TROTTO I'm your father's friend first, then a lawyer. I'll be as objective as possible.

CARL Tape record your conversations with us and Pedro.

TROTTO That, or bring a witness you select to be present at my meetings with Pedro and yourselves.

MARIA More billable hours on the clock?

TROTTO Don't you have a trusted friend who would go to both meetings?

CARL Mila. It has to fit her schedule.

MARIA Aunt Rita.

CARL She has dementia, Mom, and she's deaf.

MARIA I trust Aunt Rita.

TROTTO Pedro will bring his witness, also.

CARL Insane. No one trusts anyone. You don't even trust us. Pedro won't agree to Mila.

MARIA That's why I suggested Aunt Rita.

CARL Auntie won't remember. Pedro will accept her as a witness, then contest what she says.

TROTTO We can use the tape recorder. But if you can't agree, we'll have to go to mediation. And if you don't accept the mediator's judgment, then the will is void. I think I can safely say you must each get your own lawyers. It appears that the will is contested already.

MARIA That's an incredible leap.

TROTTO Am I right?

Silence

TROTTO My secretary will give you the names of good attorneys. I'll phone you in a week after I phone Pedro. You're sure about the order of protection?

MARIA I can't have him come to the house at all hours with my granddaughter begging for him.

CARL He's gotten so low dragging my niece into it,

Tony appears downstage right unseen to the others who talk silently in the background.

TONY'S GHOST (*to audience*) Can you blame my son, Pedro? They're sharks who refuse to agree. I put the idea in his head to go to Maria's with my granddaughter, three nights in a row around Midnight. The time of witches. I like to be helpful and move things along. Ha, ha, ha, ha.

Lights dim.

Scene 8

The evening of the same day, Maria is in her living room in a haze of pot and hash smoke. A hookah is on the table. She savors the smoke and listens to Eric Satie. Out of the haze, Tony appears dressed in a jazzy outfit. He looks youthful and refreshed.

TONY Mi amore.

Tony beckons to a startled Maria. She recovers her shock eased by her hash high. She takes his hand. They waltz awkwardly to Erik Satie.

MARIA I miss you, you bastard. Why did you leave? You were my only love.

TONY You're such a charming liar. What about that Nazi who worked at the Met Opera and fucked your brains out?

MARIA *(superior)* He was a baby Nazi, in the Hitler Youth as a kid. Right after the war, he came here with his father, a scientist.

TONY They were Nazis. I was so happy when some snitch ratted him out and they disappeared him.

MARIA How do you know?

TONY Friend in the FBI.

MARIA That was three months after we threw the hat check girl out of the cloakroom at the Argentine Club. *(happily)* And you took me against the furs.

TONY I had to. You swept me off my feet.

Tony whirls off into the arms of the ghost of Erminia, Pedro's mother. This is a flashback to the time when Tony and Maria first met at the Argentine Club. Tony is married to Erminia. They dance the tango. Maria watches with envy, gives Erminia THE EVIL EYE.

ERMINIA   What is she looking at? Puta mala. She's OVERLOOKING ME. Where's the corno portafortuna? It's in my purse. Let me get it.

TONY   She's looking at how lovely you are. You don't need that stupid charm. I'll protect you.

Going to leave, Erminia gets tangled in her steps, falls.

ERMINIA   You didn't cross me with the spiral. Coño! You led with your arm and tripped me.

TONY   Come, come. Let me help you up.

ERMINIA   Don't rush me. My hip hurts.

TONY   José, help me get her up.

ERMINIA   Leave me alone. I can do it...AGHHHH!

TONY   You're limping. Sit.

ERMINIA   Brute! I'm going to powder my nose.

MARIA *(moves to Tony)*   Such a wonderful dancer. We make a great team. I love to tango. Let's dance while she powders her thing.

TONY *(dancing with Maria)*   I'm with her.

MARIA   Not to worry. I'm an adulteress. But since I'm a lapsed Catholic, it doesn't count.

TONY   Of course, it counts.

MARIA   Not if you're modern.

◊ ⟩ The Sicilian Lighthouse ⟨ ◊

TONY I'm not.

MARIA No Italian male is old fashioned when it comes to sex. Just when it comes to his daughter.

TONY (*laughs*) Are you Italian? Argentinian?

MARIA (*stealing from the Rolling Stones song "Sympathy for the Devil"*) "Pleased to meet you. Hope you guess my name."

TONY What is it?

MARIA Maria. Named after the Black Madonna

ERMINIA (*limps to Tony and Maria*) Tony, we have to go. I think I fractured my hip.

Maria and Tony stop dancing.

TONY Are you sure? Walk on it some more to test it.

ERMINIA You want me to make it worse, you bastard? You never acknowledge my pain. Call an ambulance.

MARIA " Please allow me to introduce myself." (*Erminia doesn't get The Rolling Stones' reference.*) "I'm a 'woman' of wealth and taste."

ERMINIA Could have fooled me.

TONY That's enough. You've tickled her jealous bone.

ERMINIA You will not make me a clown to please a coño apestoso! (*to Maria*) You're a fool. He is only about his own pleasure. Never the woman's.

TONY You are a wonderful dancer. Have a good evening.

MARIA A pleasure.

Maria hands Tony a piece of paper. Tony prevents Erminia from grabbing it.

In a huff, Erminia flounces off into a haze of pot, hash and cigarette smoke.

Back in the present.

TONY   I'm glad I tipped off the FBI.

MARIA   It was you tipped them off?

TONY   I saw what I wanted that night we met. I went after it and got it. That Nazi was 35 years your senior and didn't have the balls to get it up. You were thrilled he disappeared.

MARIA   All you had to do was tell me you were dumping Erminia. I would have tipped them off myself.

They resume dancing the tango fiercely.

TONY   Mi chiquita putita. I loved you fucking two men at the same time.

MARIA   Three. There was that hot Spanish-Italian, Enrico.

TONY   That was overreaching. One of them had to go.

MARIA   You were fucking two women, il porco!

TONY   By then Erminia hated sex with me. She kicked me out of our bed the week after we danced when she found your number in my jacket pocket. I never told you to make you jealous. Ha! Ha! Ha!

Maria stops dancing with Tony. Takes a hit on the hookah. Tony snaps his fingers to change the music to the Farrell Williams song "Happy." Tony dances by himself.

MARIA Why do you tell me now, after you're dead?

TONY You have to know how I struggled to get you, and keep you, and make you jealous.

MARIA I'm impressed. You had my sexy Nazi killed for me?

TONY Not sexy. An old brute. I forgot you liked to be brutalized by sadists.

MARIA (*teasing*) Yum.

TONY Him and Erminia.

MARIA What?

TONY I killed him and Erminia.

MARIA You just said you ratted him out.

TONY I shot him. Friends and I chucked him in the East River.

He sings "Happy" by Farrell Williams to Maria.

MARIA Erminia killed herself.

TONY Nope (*dancing and singing "Happy"*).

MARIA Tony! (*She snaps her fingers. The music stops, Tony stops.*) Don't lie to me. You're dead.

TONY I'm not. It's a strange new world. I feel compelled to tell the truth.

MARIA What did you do, Tony?

TONY I got even with myself.

MARIA I mean about Erminia.

TONY I killed her for your love. I made it look like suicide.

MARIA Why did you have to ruin this interlude?

TONY Better now than later.

MARIA Why?

TONY A discovery is coming.

MARIA I don't want to know.

TONY I can't tell you. But I'm giving you warning clues out of loyalty.

MARIA Why didn't you tell me about Erminia before?

TONY Afraid I'd lose you. You'd use it as an excuse to leave me.

MARIA But you're a killer.

TONY You see what I mean? Stuff like that gets in the way.

MARIA Does this prove you really wanted me?

TONY You and your father's money. If he didn't lose it in the crash and political chaos in Argentina, then die of a stroke, we'd be in Buenos Aires now. I'd be alive and things would be so different.

MARIA But two people you cut off? Tony! Tony...

TONY Is that a problem?

MARIA No.

TONY It might be. I'm going to tell Pedro.

The Sicilian Lighthouse

MARIA You're what?

TONY I've made visitations all over. Pedro is next.

MARIA Why would you tell him?

TONY I'm really getting off on this truth thing.

MARIA You're a figment of my imagination.

TONY My conditions have changed. I'm no longer an atheist.

MARIA You aren't real.

TONY Try to put your hand through me.

MARIA No. You're a bad spirit. Something horrible will happen if I try.

TONY I'm solid substance, but not here. Go figure.

MARIA You're here because you want something. You always want something.

TONY Just like the good ole days. I want to make amends. I admit I killed my first born's mother.

MARIA But you did it out of love for me.

TONY Maria. How you trick yourself. That's not love.

MARIA Pedro's an atheist.

TONY All the more reason to believe I'm real, when I show up and tell him the truth.

MARIA This is a bad time. Tell him in a year.

TONY I've been leaving clues. I show up to whoever receives me. Pedro will be a breakthrough. My first atheist convert.

MARIA What about our granddaughter?

TONY I've seen her five times. We have great conversations. She told her father. He's taking her to a shrink.

MARIA You're frightening.

TONY I'm gentle. I tell jokes. I'm telling Pedro because Erminia is pissed, though she's enjoying spooking her Argentine family at parties.

MARIA Please, Tony. You loved me once. Don't tell him.

TONY What will you give me not to tell him?

MARIA Sex?

TONY Only for special occasions. Something else.

MARIA The will?

TONY I don't like how it's going.

MARIA But YOU wrote the will! Tell Trotto.

TONY Too late.

MARIA He's your friend.

TONY We were atheists together. I don't want to ruin his world view by showing up. Too early for his breakthrough.

MARIA Bargain with Carl.

TONY He's too dense. I can't get through to him. Besides he has nothing to bargain for. You have everything.

◊ } The Sicilian Lighthouse { ◊

MARIA I'll have nothing because we're contesting the will.

TONY No you're not. Give Pedro the house.

MARIA How will I live?

TONY With your sister in Buenos Aires…

MARIA After all those years putting up with your craziness and the wise guys, I get nothing?

TONY And the insurance money.

MARIA You can't disinherit your wife.

TONY I'm dead. I can do what I please. I can persuade you to give up everything, voluntarily. YOU can disinherit YOURSELF! Ha, ha, ha.

MARIA I won't make myself destitute. You're abandoning me twice.

TONY The least I can do for justice. You'll have 20% of the restaurant.

MARIA Forget the restaurant.

TONY He'll sue for everything after I tell him I killed his mother. He'll make sure you get nothing, even if he loses everything.

MARIA Sei un mostro. Mostro!

Tony disappears in a cloud of smoke.

MARIA Tony, sorry. Tony? I meant un fenomeno.

Tony reappears in another smokey cloud.

TONY Now, we can have sex.

MARIA Now?

TONY Nothing has changed. I will tell him we murdered his mother, unless you give up the house and insurance money. With it he'll make a success of the restaurant.

MARIA He doesn't know the first thing about running that hell hole. He'll throw the money away.

TONY I know you're mad and upset. Good! You always fuck better when you're enraged.

Tony passionately kisses her, as smoke envelopes them and the lights dim.

Scene 9

It's one hour later in the living room of Maria's house where an empty bottle of wine, glasses, hookah, and remains of hash and pot are on a table. Carl and Mila enter.

CARL We'll tell her what we're thinking.

MILA We can't, Carl. Not yet.

MARIA (*screams from the bedroom*) Oh, oh. Mi fuerte. I never knew that was possible.

CARL Hmpfff. She didn't waste any time. The rosaries on the coffin aren't even cold...una coneja.

MARIA Ahhhh.

MILA Let's go upstairs and come down in an hour.

CARL No! (*checks the pot, hookah, wine, hash remains*) Looks like they had quite a party.

Carl sits by the weed, hash, hookah, etc.

MILA Your mother smokes hash?

CARL Tony kept her in weed for her nerves. She's gotten worse.

Tony comes out of the bedroom fastening his belt. He's unseen by Carl and Mila.

TONY (*over his shoulder to Maria*) Someone's here to see you. Tell him, or I'll have Pedro lay it on him, along with a few wise guys to make the point clear.

CARL (*examining the hash*) This hash is expensive.

MILA   Did you just see the bedroom door open and close?

CARL   No. (*holds up hash pipe*) Want some?

TONY (*waves his hand in Carl's face, as Carl rolls a joint*) Nothing! No sensitivity. How can you be a filmmaker? You can't see your own father's ghost. You moron!

MILA (*seeing Tony, who leers at her, seductively*)   Argh, argh, ah…(*fainting*).

TONY   She should be the film artiste, NOT YOU!

Carl doesn't hear or see Tony. Tony disappears. Carl kneels by Mila.

CARL   Mila! Mila!

MARIA (*comes out of the bedroom dressed in a sexy, silk robe*) When did you get here? What happened?

CARL   Mila fainted. Hope she's not pregnant. Get the smelling salts.

MARIA   We don't have any. I have something better.

Maria leaves, then comes back with a glass of water.

CARL   Mila, can you hear me? Mila. (*to Maria*) Water?

MARIA (*sprinkles Mila with water*)   Relax. She's probably got low blood sugar. A problem for older women.

When the sprinkling doesn't work, Maria throws the entire glass in her face.

CARL   Call the ambulance.

MARIA   She'll come around.

CARL She fell, collapsed and hit her head! Call an ambulance.

TONY'S VOICE She'll come to in a minute. I'm talking to her.

MARIA One more minute.

Carl takes out his phone and punches in 911.

TONY Take the phone, Maria.

Maria takes Carl's phone.

CARL What the hell are you doing?

MARIA Wait, thirty more seconds. I don't want sirens and flashing lights. The neighbors.

CARL What's going on with you? It's that guy you got in there. You're maniacal!

Carl goes to the bedroom, looks in.

MARIA There's no one. You're imagining things.

MILA (*exactly 30 seconds later, sitting up*) Oh, what happened?

CARL (*kneeling next to her*) You collapsed. Are you pregnant and not telling me about our son?

MILA Not true, and what if I didn't? Oh, I remember. I saw your dad.

MARIA You saw Tony?

TONY'S VOICE She saw no one. Convince her.

MARIA You saw no one.

MILA (*to Carl*) Did you hear a rumble, like thunder?

MARIA You have a concussion, hearing and seeing things.

MILA It was Tony. He was here. You didn't see him?

CARL Mila, please. Not now.

MARIA (*whispers to an invisible Tony*) I'm telling him about us.

MILA (*excited*) I resurrected him. It worked. I resurrected him. I'm a prayer success. (*gets up, joyfully claps her hands*)

CARL We laid him in the grave...

MARIA Tony is a spirit. He visits us, but you're too dense to notice.

CARL An evil spirit. Not a good spirit. A vengeful, lying spirit. I don't wanna see him.

MARIA Mi amore is a good man. He's come back to help me.

MILA See? Your mother sees him, too.

CARL You've both gone over the edge.

MARIA If going over the edge means having fantastic sex with a resurrected spirit, I'm a fulfilled woman. Bring it on, coño!

CARL Dad is gone. This is the very essence of grief. Don't feed into this Mila.

MILA He's resurrected. My timing was a bit off, supposed to be before he was embalmed and buried, but he looks...

MARIA REFRESHED!	**MILA** REFRESHED!

MARIA Your father and I have a blood bond. I have to do his bidding. I summoned him with my desire, and he came, he came, HE CAME.

MILA (*laughs*)   What fun!!!

CARL Bidding? What did he tell you to do? This is your imagination. You're lonely.

MARIA Tony is with us now, watching.

Carl looks around afraid. Mila looks around.

MILA Nah, I don't see him.

MARIA He comes in and out like a cool breeze on a hot day.

CARL Dad's dead and we're not going to use the Ouija board or go to a medium. He's staying dead.

MILA You can't keep a resurrected spirit down when it's my resurrection.

CARL Christ!

MARIA Tony's changed the plans.

CARL Don't agree with her. You saw nothing.

MILA He appears to all who wish it.

CARL Don't go to the dark side, Mila.

MARIA May I speak to my son, alone?

CARL No. I want her with me. Speak to us both.

MARIA She saw Tony. She agrees with me. It's two against one. It will be worse for you.

CARL Mila and I have something to tell you.

MILA Not now after this wonder, this miracle. I'm a resurrector. This may be a new career plan for me. I'll go to hospitals.

MARIA Take your plan upstairs, Mila, like a good girl.

CARL You can speak in front of Mila. She's family. We're getting married.

MARIA That changes things?

CARL I'm not going to Buenos Aires.

MARIA That's right, because you're helping Pedro run The Sicilian Lighthouse.

CARL You're crazy! What was in that dope you're smoking? If you got it from Tony's friends, it's cut with crack! No wonder.

MARIA Mila, please? Here are the keys. You know how to make yourself comfortable. And after we're done, you two can have a pleasant fuck. Not as good as with my resurrected Tony, but nice.

Mila takes the keys, looks at both of them, leaves.

MARIA It's like I have a new purpose in life. Maybe I'll write my memoirs. It'll be a best seller. *Love and the Afterlife. How to Have Fantastic Sex With a Ghost.*

CARL I can't talk to you (*turns to go upstairs*).

TONY'S VOICE (*angry*) Sit down, YOU ARTISTE!

CARL You recorded him? How sad!!

TONY'S VOICE (*furious*) Sit! Down!

CARL Turn that recorder off. (*looks around the room*) Where is it?

TONY'S VOICE I never got you and you never got me. Now, I'm making up for lost time. Sit your ass down.

MARIA Mi amore. Show yourself, or he won't believe.

TONY'S VOICE All that church resurrection stuff was to get into Mila's pants. He's the fucking atheist, not Pedro!

MARIA You appeared to Pedro? But I made a deal with you not to visit him.

TONY'S VOICE It's really wacky. You think you have power in life? You got nada. Zero. Zilch. Don't know if you're coming or going most of the time. But when you're dead...the sky's the limit. You get to do what you want. With no one breathing down your neck.

CARL (*to the voice*) You're not Dad. You're one of those, one of those (*snaps fingers in recognition*) familiar spirits. Dad never said three sentences to me.

TONY'S VOICE I told ya, I'm making up for lost time.

MARIA Tony amore, did you see Pedro?

TONY'S VOICE Of course. I told him EVERYTHING!

MARIA It's a double cross!

TONY'S VOICE You always were tricked by great sex. This time, I topped my own performance. Ha, ha, ha, ha.

Lights flicker. Tony disappears. Maria sits on the sofa and finishes the wine in the glass, then puts her head in her hands.

MARIA Mi hijo. Nosotros estamos en la mierda.

CARL Stop doing the drugs. It's making you crazy.

Lights dim on Maria and Carl talking. After a beat lights rise on the upstairs apartment with Mila and Carl. Carl smokes the joint he rolled. Mila hands him a glass of wine.

CARL Pedro's coming here.

MILA Did you see Tony?

CARL Mom played his voice on a tape. She probably got it from an old 16 mm film we had.

MILA She's that technically sophisticated?

CARL He's dead! Mom is certifiable. Wish I could commit her.

MILA I saw him.

CARL (*strongly*) If I didn't know magician's tricks, I would fall for this BS, too. Pedro's probably in on it, or Trotto. Maybe that's who she was fucking.

MILA Then where did he go?

CARL I didn't check the bathroom shower. Damn!

MILA What did your father say?

CARL Mostly "sit down," like I was Rambo, the Schnauzer we used to have. Mom told me the bad news.

MILA (*looks at him waiting as he tries to remember*) Well? What?

CARL Tony double crossed her. Told Pedro something he wasn't supposed to. Pedro has a rage on. Mom thinks he's coming here to kill us to get revenge. Do you still have that gun at your place?

MILA I thought Tony had a hunting rifle?

CARL I busted it after he killed a fawn. I freaked. He just left Bambi to rot. I forced him to watch *The Deer Hunter*. He said De Niro was a pussy.

MILA Actually, the real De Niro is the guy in *The Deer Hunter* and no way like the guy in *Goodfellas*.

CARL I wonder if Phil will let me have that prop gun.

MILA No guns. Why is Pedro coming here?

CARL Tony whipped him up into a killing frenzy. Revenge.

MILA You mean Pedro sees Tony? Wow, Wow, Wow!

CARL No! He! Doesn't! He's an atheist. It's BS. My mom is nuts. She's paranoid and hallucinating from the drugs.

MILA Well, I saw your father, and I didn't take any drugs.

CARL Not now, Mila. I have to think. Someone's helping her. But who?

MILA If Pedro comes, tell her not to open the door.

CARL She has no will of her own.

MILA You make no sense.

CARL The drugs. She's hallucinating weird sex shit. Tony controls her pussy and her pussy controls her.

MILA You just said it's the drugs, and there's no Tony. So, he's not controlling her.

CARL I don't know what I said. Did I say that? I don't know what's happening.

MILA You've gone cuckoo.

CARL Me? You see ghosts.

MILA You hear them.

CARL A tape recorder. Magic tricks.

MILA Not helpful. I saw your father.

CARL I need a plan. Fighting ghosts is no plan. I can't rock her, off Tony double-crossing her, and Pedro's coming for revenge with a gun.

MILA Only devils double cross people. I think I resurrected a devil. Oh My God. The end of my resurrection career. The end of us.

CARL I think I know where I can get a gun.

MILA I said no guns.

CARL I heard you. Are you coming with me or are you leaving me to handle this alone?

He puts on his jacket and stares at Mila.

CARL Well?

Lights dim.

Scene 10

It is a day later in Maria's apartment. Maria sits in a haze of hash and opium smoke. The doorbell rings. She goes to the window and looks, then opens the door to Trotto.

MARIA   I'm having a party to celebrate my miserable life. Join me...

Trotto sits...looks at the illicit drugs on the coffee table. He picks up a tab of acid.

TROTTO   ORANGE SUNSHINE??? But they banned it.

MARIA   It's trending. Helps folks with their heroin and oxy addictions. But... I'm not an addict.

TROTTO   Who's your supplier?

MARIA   Friend of Tony. I'm waiting for him. He's late. He has to help me with Pedro.

TROTTO   You're waiting for Sal? Figures! He has a huge range of pharmaceuticals, some of them facsimiles or worse.

MARIA   Tony...I'm waiting for Tony.

Trotto takes the hookah and puts it in the kitchen. When he comes back, Maria lights a blunt.

TROTTO   No more black or blunts! I need you to focus, Maria. Enough of this shit!

Trotto takes the blunt, drowns it in a nearby glass of wine.

MARIA *(in a fog)*   What a pity.

Trotto shakes her.

MARIA Hey, stop man handling me.

TROTTO I'm trying to shake some sense into you. Pedro spoke to me. He's suing you.

MARIA (*ironic, fog brained*) La! La! La! What a shock!

Maria swallows an orange pill.

TROTTO You better take what I say very seriously. You listening?

MARIA Make it snappy. I'll be airborne in 5 minutes. Tony's coming with me. (*calls*) Tony, Tony. Come on baby. Mama needs you.

TROTTO Pedro was with the DA. There's a criminal investigation.

MARIA Pedro is Tony's tool. Tony's faking a double-cross. He knows I reach sexual frenzy if we're antagonists. Tony! Ven a mi, mi bruto bello.

TROTTO Tony's not behind this. There's evidence.

MARIA Of what?

TROTTO Murder.

MARIA Bullshit. Pedro's the criminal. He violated the Order of Protection, twice. Was here at 2:00 AM banging on the door, screaming he's going to kill us. Now, it's a criminal investigation? (*laughs*) Crazy, undisciplined, bastard. He never could focus on one thing.

TROTTO You and Tony hired two hit men to kill Erminia and that Nazi. One of them needs a favor from the DA. He's turned you over. They found the body in Newtown Creek with an anchor around the neck and identified it. The Mossad is very interested.

MARIA Tony confessed to me HE did it.

TROTTO When did he confess?

MARIA A few days ago. Then he told Pedro.

TROTTO Tony confessed nothing. The DA contacted Pedro.

MARIA Fairy tales. My ghost story is better. I can entice the porn and romance crowd to read my "How-To"! *Achieving Your Finest ORGASMS With a Ghost Lover."*

TROTTO What's your plan with this ghost thing? You're going to call in a medium and have Tony take the witness stand to incriminate himself and get you off the murder rap? Ah ha, ha, ha!

MARIA There IS no evidence. I didn't murder anyone.

TROTTO Why don't you get a REAL flight to Buenos Aires. Avoid the mess of a murder rap. Leave the estate up to me. If they indict you, I'll get someone to take care of it, so they don't extradite you to stand trial.

MARIA How convenient for you and Pedro. What deal did you make to get me out of the picture? Last night he threatens to kill me and Carl. You come hours later, bullying me to go to Buenos Aires, and lying about evidence against me and criminal investigations.

TROTTO Nothing like that.

MARIA Tony! Tony! I need you now! NOW!

TROTTO (*takes out his phone*) I'm calling 911. You're out of it. You're OD'ing!

MARIA I can hold my drugs. But I can't vouch for holding my guns.

Maria grabs a Beretta from under the sofa, fondles it.

I never went to target practice the way Tony and Carl did. But I'm willing to try. (*aims the gun at Trotto*) Now. Get the fuck out. I know a bluff when I hear it.

TROTTO   I'm not bluffing.

MARIA   OK. Get the fuck out anyway.

TROTTO   Are you listening? Pedro is suing you for the entire estate which is owed to the son of the murdered Erminia.

MARIA   I'll call you tomorrow, after I talk to Tony.

TROTTO   Talking to the dead without a medium? You must be the medium. Ha, ha, ha, ha.

MARIA   Yeah, I'm the woman in the middle.

Maria shoots the Beretta.

MARIA   Oh. That felt sooo good! I can get into this!

TROTTO   You crazy bitch. That grazed my shoulder. Call me when they arrest you. I know a good criminal defense attorney.

Trotto backs away toward the door.

MARIA   We'll have a chat after you're dead.

TROTTO   No reasoning with a cunt. You don't know what you're up against.

Maria shoots. Trotto flies out the door.

MARIA   Yeah. Neither do you, you pettifogger! You quack! Pettifogger...whoa, the shit that comes out of your lucid, acid brain. Mind blowing.

Maria goes into the kitchen and comes out with the hookah. She sets it up, smokes. Carl comes down from the upstairs apartment.

CARL I heard shots. You didn't hurt yourself, did you? Sometimes it misfires.

MARIA If it did, I can't feel a thing. Want some?

CARL Sons and mothers don't get high together. Too weird. What did Trotto want?

MARIA I took Orange Sunshine. The stuff that's coming outta me is wild.

CARL Where's the Beretta?

MARIA (*waves it around*) Still loaded.

She fires point blank range at Carl.

CARL (*unperturbed*) Very funny.

MARIA Trotto thought I grazed his shoulder. HA! The power of suggestion is all ya need. Not love.

She hands him the Beretta

CARL Yeah? What if they're firing real ammunition, not blanks?

Knocking at the door. Doorbell rings.

DEEP VOICE (*loud*) POLICE! Open up. We have a search warrant.

MARIA (*sucks on the hookah*) Yeah, yeah. (*to Carl*) Let me have the gun back.

CARL (*looks through the door viewer*) Get the stuff. We'll hide out upstairs. You have any air freshener?

MARIA (*laughs manically*)   Just farts. (*laughs to a crescendo*)

Carl goes into her bedroom comes out with perfume. Throws liquid in the air. He waves to get rid of hash and opium smell. The knocking and ringing are continuous.

CARL   Stinks like a Bordello. COME ON, MA!

MARIA (*looking for the gun*)   I never back down from a fight.

DEEP VOICE   POLICE! If you don't open up, we'll break down the door.

MUMBLING VOICES   Get the crowbar. Smash it in. Hurry up. Come on. Hurry!

Carl grabs drugs from the table.

CARL   Come on! I have the gun.

MARIA   Give it to me.

CARL   Get ahold of yourself. Take the hookah and black. Cops kill in situations like this.

MARIA   NOT a proud Italian-Argentinian woman they don't!

CARL   Suit yourself.

Carl, arms full, leaves for the back stairs. Maria tries to stand up, falls back.

MARIA   I have to come in for a landing before I walk.
Commotion at the door. Voices. POUNDING!

MARIA   I've never been arrested before. Might be an interesting experience.

She stands, sways, picks up the hookah.

The Sicilian Lighthouse

MARIA They'll never take me alive! I'm coming Tony!

Maria wobbles to the back stairs. Sounds of the door giving way. Three police officers with hats pulled down over their faces come into the living room. When one of them turns around, we see it is Pedro dressed as a police sergeant.

PEDRO Whew. Stinks. Maria's addiction is worse. Trotto said they were here. We'll check the basement. Then the upstairs apartments and the attic.

Lights dim.

End Act I

ACT TWO
◊
Scene 1

It is two days later at Mila's loft in Manhattan. Mila, Maria and Carl are at a table with a Ouija Board and Tarot Cards. An overhead shot of the table is projected on a screen. The board, their hands and cards are visible to the audience.

MARIA Not even BLACK?

CARL No drugs. Cold turkey.

MILA We have to contact Tony. We will, if he's real. No drug induced spirits of imagination allowed.

MARIA The sex was stupendous. You saw him. He's real.

CARL Lucinda was watching from her front window across the street. She said Pedro and his goons left. Now's the time to get back.

MILA We'll go, but not before I exorcize that demon.

MARIA Demons make the best lovers. I want him.

CARL Demons are liars. We need the truth.

MILA When you place your hands, be gentle. Fingers lightly on the planchette.

MARIA No candles or lights out darkness?

MILA Last time I had candles, the flames shot up to the ceiling. I nearly burned down this loft.

CARL Count me out.

MILA You're a part of this.

CARL I don't want to see him. I'm answering emails.

MILA We need your agreement, if we have to cast him out. Get the Bible.

CARL I don't have your faith to get rid of a bad spirit. Call me when it's over.

Carl leaves.

MARIA Can I have some wine first? I'm nervous.

MILA Fingers lightly, focus on questions. I know what Bible verses I'll use.

Mila arranges her fingers on the planchette. Maria follows. We see the projection of her hands on the planchette in the overhead shot. A beat.

MILA We call on the spirit of Tony.

Silence

MARIA Mi amore, ven acá! Ahora!

MILA Are you here? Is the spirit here?

MARIA (*excited*) It's moving. Mi amore said, "YES!"

MILA Will you answer some questions?

MARIA Do you miss me Tony? Are you happy?

MILA Yes! It's moving to yes. He's happy.

MARIA You BASTARD! Who are you with over there?

MILA It's spelling out...it's between an E and...

MARIA You're with Erminia? And having sex with me, here? Cornuta! (*stands, outraged*) How dare you!

MILA Maria, please. I thought you wanted to do this.

MARIA Let me ask the questions. (*sits, arranges her hands*) Are you happy with me, Tony?

The planchette moves wildly from side to side. Maria goes unconscious and slumps over.

MILA Carl! Carl! Your mother passed out! Carl.

CARL (*enters*) What? I don't want to see him.

MARIA DEEP VOICE You don't believe. Get out! Get out!

CARL Believe what?

SPIRIT POSSESSED MARIA Angry. I am angry. You are angry.

CARL Fuckin' A. I'm furious!

SPIRIT POSSESSED MARIA Don't say bad words. I get angrier.

CARL You left me nothing. You disinherited me, your son with the woman you loved.

SPIRIT POSSESSED MARIA I! DID! NOT!

CARL In the will. You did. Trotto read it to us.

SPIRIT POSSESSED MARIA Not the will!

MILA WOW!

CARL There's another will?

SPIRIT POSSESSED MARIA Yes!

MILA
Where?

CARL
Where?

SPIRIT POSSESSED MARIA In the place no one will look!

CARL I'm bad at riddles. Where is that?

Silence

MILA Where, Tony?

SPIRIT POSSESSED MARIA Not Tony!

CARL You're not Tony?

SPIRIT POSSESSED MARIA Nonno!!!

CARL (*proud*) Mom named me after my grandfather.

SPIRIT POSSESSED MARIA Nonno Carlo.

MILA Oh, no.

CARL What?

MILA I can't cast out grandparents. They're sacred.

CARL It's a spirit. It still could be lying.

MILA What spirit would identify as a Nonno Carlo? They wouldn't dare. It IS your grandfather.

SPIRIT POSSESSED MARIA My namesake will never be disinherited.

CARL (*enthusiastic*) Thank you Nonno, Carlo.

MILA (*ironic*) Oh. So, NOW you believe?

CARL I can't offend Nonno Carlo. He's protecting me.

SPIRIT POSSESSED MARIA Go.

CARL Where?

SPIRIT POSSESSED MARIA Go to the place where no one will look.

MILA Where, Nonno Carlo?

SPIRIT POSSESSED MARIA The safe place. The safe place. The safe place.

Maria falls on the floor. Shudders, quiets.

CARL He left just as he was going to tell us.

MILA He wants us to figure it out. We have to earn it.

CARL The story of my life.

Maria wakes up still in a trance. She gets up and walks toward the door.

CARL Mom?

MILA Stop her. She'll go into the road.

CARL Mom! Mom! (*shakes her*) She's in a trance.

MILA (*commanding*) In God's name, AWAKE!

Maria pulls away from Carl and starts to wander.

CARL Stop her. Don't let her fall. Good. OK. I'll take her now. Get a wet dish towel.

Carl sits Maria in a chair.

MILA Maria wake up. This should cool you. (*wipes her with the towel*) You're sweating.

CARL A safe place. Nonno, Nonno! Where is that?

MARIA (*awakens*) I'm burning up.

MILA The drugs are leaving her body. She feels feverish. Look she's shaking with the chills.

Carl brings a glass of water and an aspirin. He gives it to her.

CARL Here.

MARIA (*swallowing the pill*) Agh! I feel like something went through me.

CARL Nonno Carlo spoke through you.

MARIA Not Tony?

MILA No. And he didn't cheat on you.

CARL Don't worry. You still have the upper hand.

MARIA (*softly cries*) I don't. He's dead. And I'm left here without him. And no amount of opium will bring him back to me. I want to die. I want to die.

CARL (*smiles*) Things are looking brighter! She's coming to herself.

MILA Don't cry, Mom. May I call you Mom?

MARIA (*annoyed*) You're too old for me to be your mother. Maria!

MILA Maria! I'm so sorry Tony's gone (*hugs her*)

CARL Did Dad ever mention another will?

MARIA (*sniffling into a handkerchief she takes from her pocket*) No. Just that Trotto was our lawyer.

MILA Estate lawyer?

MARIA He takes care of everything. Why?

CARL Nonno Carlo said there's another will in a place where no one would look.

MARIA The house. In the basement or attic. We never went there. It's full of junk, we didn't want to deal with.

CARL You realize we've been hiding at Mila's for two days.

MARIA Pedro doesn't have a key. He needed us out of the house. Except for Lucinda recognizing Pedro, we would think we're wanted criminals. Pedro and his disguised thugs break in and look for the will. So, Trotto never got the will from Tony. Something happened.

CARL Lucinda said yellow crime scene tape is barring the front door. But they left.

As they've been talking Mila puts out the tarot cards. She turns three cards over.

MARIA If they found the will, they destroyed it by now. The fake one Trotto takes to probate. He and Pedro have a deal. The way it's written he makes a bundle if any part of the will is contested. He probably made himself the mediator, too. Whatever that spirit was, evil or good, it helped me see through Trotto.

MILA If it's an evil spirit, I'll exorcize it. We need the help of good spirits like Nonno.

CARL So if it was Nonno Carlo who came, that means Trotto is NOT the Executor of the will. Mom probably is.

MILA Look at the Tarot Cards that came up.

CARL Do we want to know this?

We see the cards projected on a screen.

MILA The past, the present the future. The Four of Cups is the Past. It stands for missed opportunities and regrets. You, your Dad. The Five of Wands is the present. Chaos, fights, conflict. And this is the future. (*Mila points to the Death Card projected on the screen.*)

CARL I'm not ready for this.

MILA It doesn't always mean death.

MARIA It's Tony's death and the original will. We have to search the house. We go in the back way like before, the side street where Mila picked us up, through the backyards.

MILA Maybe someone is still watching.

MARIA What can they do? We know the truth. The law is on our side. Fraud, impersonating cops, breaking and entering, theft, fake will.

CARL If they're watching, that means they didn't find the will.

MARIA Just in case, we'll scare them away with the Beretta.

MILA No guns. The Death card! The Death card.

CARL I'll carry the gun.

MARIA I'm a better shot than you. More convincing.

CARL Pedro's not bluffing. He'll have a real gun, real bullets this time.

MARIA Leave him and Trotto to me. (*laughs*)

As they leave, the lights dim.

Scene 2

It's three hours later at Maria's townhouse apartment in New Jersey. Mila and Carl pile boxes filled with junk to secure the front door so no one can enter.

CARL Best way to throw out stuff you don't want is to search for something you do.

MARIA (*enters with a shabby game board box*) I found our Ouija Board.

MILA How old is that?

MARIA It's my mother's. I brought it from Buenos Aires as a remembrance of my life. *(laughs)* We never used it. Oh the times, the laughter, the pain. Canyons in my heart.

CARL (*comes back from the window*) Not out there. They burned the will by now. It's over. How can we prove that will's a fraud before he goes to probate? Pedro's support gives him credibility.

MILA What if we make a fake will to fake out the fakers? Secretly tape them and get their confession, so they reveal the fraud.

MARIA (*holds up Ouija Board*) The spirits will guide us. Tony feels comfortable in his house. For that I'll have some pot.

CARL NO POT! NO SPIRITS.

MARIA You see what he's like? You're from opposite poles of the universe.

MILA That's what I love about him.

CARL (*puts his arms around her*) She's my baby.

The Sicilian Lighthouse

MARIA More like the other way around.

MILA You shouldn't be so sensitive about my age, Maria. It's fashionable for younger men to be with older women. Very chic.

MARIA I never went in for fashion. I like the old ways, the remembrance of things past. Come on Mila, Carl. We touch the spirits.

CARL I was OK at Mila's. Not here. It's dangerous. Unstable. You're still out of it. You still have acid and the other shit in your system. You look awful. Here. Take another aspirin. Meanwhile, I'll check the attic walls and floorboards. Maybe he stuffed the will behind a loose brick or board.

Carl leaves.

MARIA I like candles. (*lights a tall candle*) Come we'll use this table. Where are you going?

MILA (*comes back with a pitcher of water*) Just in case a spirit gets a bit fiery.

They position themselves with the planchette. They wait. Nothing happens.

MILA We command the spirits. Come. Where are you?

MARIA Tony, Tony. (*sings the first lines of "Mi Bruto Bello"*) "Rama en vez de flor, O en vez de hoja. Hoja en vez de petalo de rosa, Tierra firme y ruda." (*hums*)

Silence

MILA We have to ask the spirits "yes" or "no" questions.

MARIA (*cries quietly*) I want to see him. This is a shadow of our lives. I need the drugs to get me through. Where did Carl stash them? I grieve. My life, the dark clouds are coming...

MILA Mom, maybe we should do the Tarot Cards?

MARIA *(upset)* DON'T CALL ME MOM! You have a mother.

MILA She's dead.

MARIA Let's contact her. It's all the same over there.

MILA No. She didn't believe in the black arts. It's a sin.

The candle flickers and goes out. Carl rushes into the room.

CARL We have to leave. Lucinda called. They just parked on the street. They'll be coming.

MARIA They can't get in. The boxes. Where's the gun, the gun. We need the gun.

MILA No guns!

Maria frantic, gets up, searches for the gun.

CARL Never mind. I have it.

Carl shudders and trembles trying to shake off bugs.

CARL *(loudly)* Argh! Ewww. Stop!

MILA What's going on?

CARL ARGH...NO. That's enough...stabbing, bleeding ARGHH ROOOOWWRRR.

MARIA He's wild. Grab his arms. Calm him.

Mila gets up overturns the Ouija Board.

MILA Come here. Darling, be calm.

Carl shakes her off. He takes punches from an invisible being, and he punches back. He takes blows. He is knocked down on the floor, then gets up and fights possession by the spirit.

CARL (TONY'S VOICE) Coño. You never could take a punch.

CARL (REAL CARL) Chinga tu madre.

Carl shadow boxes with himself, fighting with the invisible spirit of Tony, who punches him back and tries to possess him. First, he takes a punch. Then he recovers and punches Tony. This continues until Maria interferes.

MARIA Mi amore, mi amore.

Maria caresses, massages Carl.

MILA Mom, know your place! That's your SON!

MARIA It's Tony's voice, even if it isn't his hair.

CARL (AS CARL) Get her off me!

MARIA I feel it's his soul, my same self. We are one. Don't reject me, mi Antonio! Por favor!

CARL (AS TONY) Mi donna, mi Bellissima donna.

MARIA Te adoro.

CARL (AS HIMSELF) (*fights possession*) Off, off, off. EWWW...

MILA Tony? Are you Tony?

CARL (ANOTHER SPIRIT) Never Tony.

MARIA Tony, are you in there? We have so much to do. No sex, I promise, mi amore.

Carl collapses on the floor. Maria on her knees slaps his face. Carl's eyes open.

CARL (ANOTHER SPIRIT TAKES OVER)   YOU! ARE! FALLEN!

MILA   Who are you?

CARL (SPIRIT) Tony's priest!

MARIA   Tony, don't leave. I'll kill myself. *(realizes)* Tony doesn't have a priest.

MILA   Who are you?

Carl gets up, dances around shadow boxing like an ersatz Muhammed Ali.

CARL (BLACK SPIRIT*)*   I'm on a mission from God.

MARIA   What?

CARL (BLACK SPIRIT)   Say what? Say what? Say what?

MILA   Questions! Ask him questions!

CARL (BLACK SPIRIT)   SAY WHAT? SAY WHAT? SAY WHAT?

MILA   Who are you?

CARL (ITALIAN SPIRIT)   Zio, Zio, Zio!

MILA   Uncle?

CARL (ITALIAN SPIRIT)   Zio, Zio, Zio!

MARIA   Tony's brother?

CARL (ITALIAN SPIRIT)   Zio Si. Tony, no!

MARIA   Chi sei?

CARL (ITALIAN SPIRIT)   Zio, si! Tony, no!

MARIA   Father Luciano? His great uncle?

CARL (FATHER LUCIANO)   Si. Capa tosta.

MILA   Where is Nonno Carlo? Send him.

CARL (LUCIANO) (*resumes shadow boxing, dancing*)   Sta pranzando.

MARIA   Having lunch? Do you know where the will is?

CARL (LUCIANO)   Posto sicuro, posto sicuro.

MARIA   Safe place.

MILA   Nonno is with the will?

CARL (LUCIANO)   Posto sicuro. Nessuno vede.

MARIA   Safe place. No one sees. Zio Luciano, cosa stai mangiando?

MILA   Of course, Nonno's eating.

CARL (LUCIANO)   Una salsiccia grassa.

MARIA   Morcillas?

CARL   E vero!

MILA	**MARIA**
The Sicilian Lighthouse	The Sicilian Lighthouse

Carl drops to the floor senseless. The candle lights up by itself. Carl's phone rings. Maria tries to wake Carl. Mila clicks on the phone.

TROTTO   We're having sandwiches at Lucinda's. Pedro's coming over there. Be good hosts and offer him a whiskey neat. We're ready to negotiate. (*clicks off phone*)

There is loud knocking on the door.

PEDRO   Open up. It's over. There's no other will.

CARL (*awakening*)   Uhgg. Uhgg.

MARIA (*kneels by Carl*)   Carl, get up. We need you. Carl! Carl!

Maria goes to the kitchen for water and comes back.

MILA (*calls to Pedro*)   Wait. We have to move the boxes from the door.

PEDRO   You have five minutes. My guys will be pissed, if you take them from Lucinda's yummy buffet.

MILA   Coming.

She pretends to move the boxes, makes sounds of lifting and straining. Maria kneels next to Carl who sits up shaking his head, dazed.

MARIA   Here's some water. After a possession you're usually thirsty. Where's the Beretta? Pedro's at the door.

CARL   AGG. Aching. (*drinks water*) We have to think of a plan.

MILA   Hurry up, I can't stall him. He'll bring his thugs.

PEDRO   You have one minute left. In fact. I'm calling my guys now. They're coming. Open the fuck up!

CARL Mom, take Pedro to the attic. Say the real will is behind the brick I was pulling out. Say I collapsed from a possession. Then run down. I'll lock him in.

MILA Coming. There's a lot of boxes. (*moves boxes*) Be right there.

PEDRO Come on, guys. Push! Push!

We hear sounds of pushing and grunting. Mila moves boxes. At the last box, she opens the door. Pedro and guys fall into the room. Carl lies down "unconscious."

MILA Oh, careful, you'll hurt yourselves.

PEDRO You can go. I got this. So. You didn't find it either? That's because there IS no will.

MILA Then why are you hunting us down and stalking us like rats?

PEDRO Trotto and I are responsible and diligent.

MILA You mean fraudulent.

PEDRO I'm not keen on him nickel and diming us if we don't agree. He plans to take it all in lawyer's and mediator's fees.

MILA His will is a fake.

PEDRO Prove it!

MILA You're here, aren't you? You think there's another will. If you find it, and give it to him, he'll destroy it. We'll all lose out.

PEDRO Maybe yes, maybe no. (*pause*) What happened to Carl?

MARIA We asked the Ouija Board some questions, and it got fucked up. Spirits possessed Carl.

PEDRO What did they say? (*to Carl*) Get up!

Pedro kicks Carl.

MARIA Don't hurt him. It's a dangerous time. He can have a heart attack when the spirits leave. That's why he collapsed, so they go out gently.

PEDRO Get him up, or I kick him in the balls.

MARIA A spirit said the will is in the attic.

PEDRO We looked up there, in the boxes, everywhere. It's not there.

MARIA It's behind a brick that's sticking out from the wall.

PEDRO Show me.

MARIA I can't. I have to be with him in case he dies like Tony. (*pretends to cry*)

PEDRO Mila stay with him. Let's go.

Pedro kicks Carl in the side. Carl doesn't react.

MARIA Figlio di una mignotta

PEDRO What? (*laughs*) Maybe he already had a heart attack. Come on. You go first.

MILA You're a piece of shit you know that?

Maria leads Pedro through the attic door.

MILA (*furious, calls at the door*) You're a bastard.

Mila helps Carl up, who is holding his side. He limps to the attic door and stands behind it.

MILA (*yells*) You've always resented Carl. His Dad loved his mom and him more than you.

CARL (*whispering*) Shshhh! Get ready.

Maria comes racing down the stairs.

MARIA Quick, quick. He grabbed me, ripped my dress.

Carl locks the door. In moments we hear PEDRO pounding and cursing throughout.

CARL I'll get furniture to block it. Mila take care of the boxes at the door. Mom call the police. Tell them there's a break in. That will stall him and give us a head start to The Lighthouse.

Pedro screams curses in Spanish. Carl moves furniture. Mila moves the boxes. Maria punches in numbers to 911.

MARIA (*frantic*) Hello? I'm desperate. They're trying to break in. My door's busted. I locked up one of the robbers in my attic. The others are coming. The address is...

Lights dim.

Scene 3

One hour later, The Sicilian Lighthouse. Carl, Mila and Maria enter the restaurant.

MARIA Hijo, make me a drink.

CARL They're coming! How can you drink at a time like this?

MARIA We've locked the outer door. Pedro doesn't have a key.

CARL Not on my life.

MARIA My head is drilling. Little men are ripping through concrete up here (*points to her head*).

MILA What did he mean by the safe place?

MARIA (*yells*) Hijo! Por favor, tu madre pobrecito.

MILA (*calls spirits*) Zio Luciano. Nonno Carlo? A Donde?

MARIA Italiano, Mila.

MILA (*calls the spirits*) Dove, Nonno Carlo. The safe place Zio? Zio? Dove?

CARL (*finishes making the drink*) Here!

MARIA (*drinks*) You look so good at that bar, like you're in control.

CARL (*realizes*) Maybe safe place means the restaurant safe?

Carl leaves through a side door.

MILA Zio, Zio Luciano? Dove?

MARIA (*sipping her drink*) Posto sicuro. Posto sicuro.

We hear a commotion. Carl emerges. Trotto is behind him, a gun pointing at his back.

TROTTO I already checked the safe. Not there.

CARL You stole it.

TROTTO Ah, ha, ha. You want to search me?

MILA How did you get in?

MARIA Like any weasel, they burrow and burrow and claw and scratch.

TROTTO I own the place. Tony ran it into the ground for me. A losing proposition is always a great way to launder money.

ALONZO (*comes in with a small plastic gas can*) About done in there, boss.

TROTTO (*yells*) It can't look obvious. I told you not gasoline. Cooking oil. COOKING OIL!

ALONZO (*whining*) I just sprinkled a little.

TROTTO YOU'RE A MORON!

MILA You're not being politically correct.

TROTTO Shut up.

CARL That gun's not loaded.

TROTTO It isn't? (*shoots light fixture which explodes*). Sprinkle olive oil to camouflage the gasoline. Do I have to do everything myself?

Alonzo leaves.

MARIA Oh my God. Oh my God. Oh my God. Oh my God.

MILA	**TROTTO**	**CARL**
WHAT?	WHAT?	WHAT????

MARIA (*a bit high*) Olive oil. Reminds me of the time Tony and I made love in the kitchen and the yummy, cold-pressed olive oil was our lubricant.

CARL EWWW, Mom.

TROTTO Sit! All of you!

Trotto motions with the gun for them to sit.

MARIA (*leaves for the kitchen*) That was the best olive oil. A shame to use it to start an insurance fire.

TROTTO Stop, Maria. Or I'll shoot Carl.

MARIA *(calls his bluff)* Go ahead. He needs toughening up.

Trotto shoots Carl in the foot. He falls out of the chair. Throughout the scene he whimpers in pain. Mila goes to him, tries to help him.

CARL AGHHHH!!! AGHHH!!! MOM! HE'S NOT BLUFFING!

MILA (*yells*) You bastard. You hurt him. You are one, lunatic, fringe fuck.

TROTTO (*yells*) Alonzo, bring Maria back here.

CARL AGH! AGH! (*rocks back and forth*)

TROTTO Stop whining. I just nicked your big toe.

MILA You know how painful stubbing a big toe is? Did you blow it off? MORON! MORON! MORON!

A gallon jug of green liquid flies out the kitchen entrance.

TROTTO (*yells*) Alonzo? What the FUCK?

Alonzo comes out of the kitchen followed by Maria with a gun pointed at his back.

ALONZO Boss, I can't hit an older woman. She looks like my mother.

TROTTO Drop the gun, Maria.

MARIA Fuck you, Trotto. You are one disappointment. You probably aren't even Tony's lawyer.

ALONZO Boss! She set the stuff on fire.

TROTTO What?

ALONZO Before I could cover the gasoline. She grabs the olive oil from Tuscany and, and...

MARIA He dies and then you die. Put the gun down or we all burn.

CARL (*yells*) I'm already in pain. No more shooting. Put out the fire!

MILA Shoot him, Maria. It's self-defense. Shoot!

Smoke comes out of the kitchen entry way.

TROTTO It was supposed to be a small kitchen fire. (*yells*) Outta my way.

Trotto runs to the kitchen. Maria shoots him at the same time he shoots at her and hits Alonzo, who blocks his aim at Maria. Alonzo takes the hit. Trotto shoots Maria, as she shoots back. Trotto falls into the kitchen entranceway. Crawls in. Smoke intensifies.

CARL   Mom. Mom!

MILA   Don't try to stand, Carl. I'm holding her.

ALONZO   Puta de madre. Puta de madre. I'm hit, I'm hit.

MARIA (*laughs*)   I got him! I got him!

CARL (*in agony*)   That's not the Beretta

MARIA (*maniacal*)   Ah, ha, ha, ha. I told you to leave Trotto and Pedro to me.

Maria is trembling. She goes down on one knee, holding onto a table that crashes down.

MILA   You're hit bad.

Mila tries to help Maria up. Alonzo crawls to the front of the restaurant to the door. Smoke pours out of the kitchen.

ALONZO (*in pain*)   I'm not burning for that bastard.

MARIA   A flesh wound.

PEDRO (*at the front door, pounding*)   Open up! Open up. I know you're in there!

TROTTO (*screams from the kitchen*)   Alonzo. Bring the other fire extinguisher. I can't put it out. I'm hurt. COME! HELP! ME!

ALONZO   All the shit I did for you at MINIMUM WAGE? (*yells*) GO FUCK YOURSELF.

◊ ⟩ The Sicilian Lighthouse ⟨ ◊

MARIA (*in Mila's arms, fatefully*) We're in hell or maybe this is heaven? Tony! I'm coming. A perfect ending, I'm bleeding to death. Help Carl out of here. Let Pedro in. He can burn with Trotto. Tony come get me, Tony????

MILA No. I'm helping you. I pray resurrection, resurrection. You are healed, healed!

MARIA Here. The will. (*coughs loudly*)

Maria grabs at her heart.

MILA Mom! MOM! No, no.

MARIA (*loudly*) Don't call me Mom! (*coughs*) This is where Tony died. It's where I die.

CARL (*crawls to Maria*) Mom! Stay! Stay!

MARIA (*takes a white envelope out of the bosom of her dress, gasping with rough breaths*) Tony put the original will in the hidden compartment under our table where we always made love after closing. I was the only one who knew about "our safe place." I remembered the olive oil, from Tuscany. Very precious lubricant helps with love making. (*passes out*)

At the entrance, Alonzo opens the door for Pedro. In pain Alonzo struggles to leave as Pedro helps him up then comes inside.

PEDRO What the fuck?

MILA Trotto and that thug set fire to the kitchen. Help him. You want the restaurant? (*yells*) Take the extinguisher and put it out!

Pedro runs to the kitchen. We hear a commotion and spraying of fire extinguishers and Pedro's and Trotto's voices. Then we hear sirens in the distance.

TROTTO Over there! There! Don't spray it at an angle, you'll spread it.

PEDRO Fuck, it's hot. Great job, Trotto. You wanted a small insurance fire, you got a blaze. Fuck! Damn!

Sirens are blaring at the front door.

CARL I called 911 when Mom distracted Trotto.

Mila leans over Maria's body to get a pulse.

MILA Be healed! Be resurrected! Maria? Maria? MOM!

CARL (*holds Maria's head*) They'll revive her. Get the door for EMT and the firemen. Hurry, hurry! Tell them there's a dying woman in here. (*yells*) Bring the oxygen, the stretcher.

Mila runs to the door. We hear Mila's voice explaining. A Fireman comes in with a hose. EMT comes in and helps Maria.

Lights dim.

Scene 4

It is months later and The Sicilian Lighthouse is in the process of renovations. Mila and Carl enter and go over to Pedro who is dressed in coveralls and is supervising workmen.

CARL *(takes out a contract)* Here you go. Signed over to you, debts paid. That's your inheritance.

PEDRO Beautiful. Trotto signed it over with no hassles?

CARL He's happy to walk away without looking back. If he tries to fight us, he could end up in jail for arson, insurance fraud, estate fraud. This cruddy restaurant, in exchange for his new life of crime elsewhere is worth it.

PEDRO You'll see. After the renovations are complete, it will be shining.

CARL Your cousin Matthew is a dynamite lawyer.

MILA Yeah. Very thorough.

PEDRO We are so fortunate. He handled the estate and everything else for a decent fee.

MILA And he knew how to get rid of Trotto. He's physically handicapped from the shooting, but his mind is like a steel trap. If he ever regrets the deal we made, Matthew will make sure criminal charges are filed against him. No statute of limitations on murder.

CARL I think mom shot first.

MILA He shot you. She shot him in self-defense and wounded him. He shot back with a mortal wound. A jury would have to decide. I thought you didn't have the heart to pursue it as a part of the deal? It won't bring her back.

Silence. Carl turns away, holding back emotion. Mila puts her arms around him.

MILA   Better keep him dangling in uncertainty. Anyway, Matthew's firm is calling for him to be disbarred in New York State because of his machinations with the fake will. He'll probably go to Jersey to practice. Lots of shysters over there who can use a lawyer in a wheelchair to get sympathy.

PEDRO   I hope he and his goons don't come back here for revenge.

MILA   Any problem, tell Matthew and the law firm (*hands Pedro a card*). Any problem, any threats, then he sets in motion a series of events that will land him in jail. It's in a contract that they made Trotto sign. He reneges, he's toast, every which way but loose!

PEDRO   Thanks, Mila. I thought you were Carl's bitch. You're one hellova woman. You gotta marry her.

CARL   Going away.

PEDRO   What?

MILA   Italy and Sicily.

PEDRO   What?

CARL   We're getting married in the same church Nonno Carlo and Nonna Emma were married before they went to Buenos Aires.

PEDRO   Congratulations. Where you gonna live?

CARL   Maybe at Mila's, once Mom's house is sold.

MILA   My place will be his base to work on his films.

CARL   Good thing Tony and Mom squirreled away thousands in cash. It was in packets in the secret compartment under the table.

(*laughs*) They made frenzied love on top of the table excited by thoughts of their retirement stash underneath.

MILA   Trotto didn't know?

CARL   He taught Dad how to skim from the profits. Then, he got crazy thinking Dad was stealing from him, so he didn't pay the rent on the restaurant. It's why the lease was owed, and we were in trouble.

PEDRO   Thanks, Carl. I mean you didn't have to. The will left everything to your mom and by extension, you. You didn't have to give me the restaurant after the lease and damages were paid as part of the deal we made with Trotto.

CARL   You're my only family in the US. Mom and Dad are gone. I love my niece and want to have a part in her life as her uncle. The past is history. We'll never really know what happened. Tony and Maria were big story tellers. It's important we live in the present. We have one enemy. What was mom's word? A PETTIFOGGER! Trotto's gotta stay away or be criminally charged. You love the restaurant. I hated it. You get to make it the place you want. I get to make my films.

MILA   Glad criminal charges are one of Matthew's conditions.

PEDRO   Sorry for those things I said. I was hurt and angry.

CARL   I gave it back just as bad. We were both bastards.

MILA   From now on, there's an open door with us.

PEDRO   For me too.

MARIA   After we return from Italy, can we come in for morcillas and margaritas?

PEDRO   Any time. Let me show you the specs for the kitchen renovations.

CARL   Hey bro, what are you gonna call this place after it's renovated?

PEDRO   Come on, bro? It's our legacy. The Sicilian Lighthouse!

Pedro, Mila and Carl look at the plans that Pedro spread out on a table. Standing together down left are Nonno Carlo, Maria and Tony. They each hold a wine glass with wine. The others don't know the spirits are looking at them. Tony has his arm around Maria.

NONNO CARLO   Cin cin. (*clicks glasses with Maria and Tony*) a faro Siciliano.

TONY and MARIA   Cin Cin! The Sicilian Lighthouse!

They all drink the wine and raise their glasses to their progeny who are busy looking at the plans for the new Sicilian Lighthouse Ristorante.

NONNO CARLO   Tutto bene. Mangiamo!

Spirits disappear and the lights dim..

THE END

AUTHOR'S NOTES

The Sicilian Lighthouse is a stylized play of the imagination. As such, it is fictional, and it is original. The characters and dialogue take inspiration from the playwright's own life.

www.ingramcontent.com/pod-product-compliance
Lightning Source LLC
Chambersburg PA
CBHW072213070526
44585CB00015B/1318